Kanye West

Other books in the People in the News series:

Kanye West

by Barbara Sheen

LUCENT BOOKS
A part of Gale, Cengage Learning

GALE
CENGAGE Learning™

Detroit • New York • San Francisco • New Haven, Conn • Waterville, Maine • London

ROX8644736

GALE
CENGAGE Learning™

LIBRARY OF CONGRESS CATALOGING-IN-PUBLICATION DATA

Sheen, Barbara
 Kanye West / by Barbara Sheen.
  p. cm. — (People in the news)
 Includes bibliographical references and index.
 ISBN 978-1-4205-0159-9 (hardcover)
 1. West, Kanye—Juvenile literature. 2. Rap musicians—United
States—Biography—Juvenile literature. I. Title.
 ML3930.W42S54 2009
 782.421649092—dc22
 [B]
                                                                    2009013457

Lucent Books
27500 Drake Rd
Farmington Hills MI 48331

ISBN-13: 978-1-4205-0159-9
ISBN-10: 1-4205-0159-3

Printed in the United States of America
1 2 3 4 5 6 7 13 12 11 10 09

Printed by Bang Printing, Brainerd, MN, 1st Ptg., 08/2009

Contents

782.421649
S539z Wk

Fame and celebrity are alluring. People are drawn to those who walk in fame's spotlight, whether they are known for great accomplishments or for notorious deeds. The lives of the famous pique public interest and attract attention, perhaps because their experiences seem in some ways so different from, yet in other ways so similar to, our own.

Newspapers, magazines, and television regularly capitalize on this fascination with celebrity by running profiles of famous people. For example, television programs such as *Entertainment Tonight* devote all their programming to stories about entertainment and entertainers. Magazines such as *People* fill their pages with stories of the private lives of famous people. Even newspapers, news-magazines, and television news programs frequently delve into the lives of well-known personalities. Despite the number of articles and programs, few provide more than a superficial glimpse at their subjects.

Lucent's People in the News series offers young readers a deeper look into the lives of today's newsmakers, the influences that have shaped them, and the impact they have had in their fields of endeavor and on other people's lives. The subjects of the series hail from many disciplines and walks of life. They include authors, musicians, athletes, political leaders, entertainers, entrepreneurs, and others who have made a mark on modern life and who, in many cases, will continue to do so for years to come.

These biographies are more than factual chronicles. Each book emphasizes the contributions, accomplishments, or deeds that have brought fame or notoriety to the individual and shows how that person has influenced modern life. Authors portray their subjects in a realistic, unsentimental light. For example, Bill Gates—the cofounder and chief executive officer of the software giant Microsoft—has been instrumental in making personal computers the most vital tool of the modern age. Few dispute his business savvy, his perseverance, or his technical expertise, yet critics say he is ruthless in his dealings with competitors, and he driven more by his desire to maintain Microsoft's dominance in the computer industry than by an interest in furthering technology.

In these books, young readers will encounter inspiring stories about real people who achieved success despite enormous obstacles. Oprah Winfrey—the most powerful, most watched, and wealthiest woman on television today—spent the first six years of her life in the care of her grandparents while her unwed mother sought work and a better life elsewhere. Her adolescence was colored by promiscuity, pregnancy at age fourteen, rape, and sexual abuse.

Each author documents and supports his or her work with an array of primary and secondary source quotations taken from diaries, letters, speeches, and interviews. All quotes are footnoted to show readers exactly how and where biographers obtained their information and provide guidance for further research. The quotations enliven the text by giving readers eyewitness views of the life and accomplishments of each person covered in the People in the News series.

In addition, each book in the series includes photographs, an annotated bibliography, a time line, and a comprehensive index. For both the casual reader and the student researcher, the People in the News series offers insight into the lives of today's news makers—people who shape the way we live, work, and play in the modern age.

Music
for Everyone

Kanye West is one of the most successful and popular hip-hop artists in the world. His music, which he writes, produces, and performs, is fresh and different. Yet, when he was first starting out as a performing artist, very few people believed that he would become a superstar. West, however, believed in himself and the power of his music.

Time has proven West right. West's words and beats have taken hip-hop in a new direction. This is not the first time hip-hop has changed. It has gone through many stages in its history.

Hip-hop began as dance music in the 1970s. Early hip-hop performers were a diverse group who came from various social classes and racial groups. Their raps dealt with a wide variety of topics, some serious and some nonsensical, but it was the beat that was most important.

Over time hip-hop lyrics became more serious and the performers less diverse. Most were African American men who grew up in poverty in America's inner cities. Before becoming celebrities, many had engaged in criminal activities to earn a living. Their music, which became known as gangsta rap, reflected their experiences. It often glorified crime, violence, promiscuity, drug use, materialism, and sexism.

Many artists often continued their criminal activities even after becoming successful. Socially unacceptable behavior raised a rapper's popularity with fans. Even hip-hop performers who were not involved in illegal activities pretended they were lawbreakers.

Kanye West has taken hip-hop in a new direction with his words and beats.

Although gangsta rap was, and still is, a popular and artistic form of music, by the start of the twenty-first century some hip-hop fans were ready for a change. The lifestyle gangsta rap portrayed offended them, and/or they felt that the music had little to do with their lives. According to 1980s hip-hop legend Darryl McDaniels of the rap group Run DMC, "this past decade it seems like hip-hop has mostly been about parties and guns and women … the music had nothing to do with me."[1]

A New Face

In 2004 Kanye West changed rap music. Although he was influenced by gangsta rap, he was not a traditional gangsta rapper, nor did he try to represent himself as one. He did not grow up in poverty and was never involved in criminal activities. He was a middle-class college dropout. His raps reflected his quirky sense of humor and the middle-class values, Christian ethics, and social activism that his family instilled in him. His beats, too, were unique. Author and hip-hop expert Jake Brown explains, "West had no interest in being part of thug life, rather he sought to preach and project a more mainstream message and image that was not radical by nature."[2]

West's lyrics and beats created a new form of hip-hop that was edgy, socially relevant, witty, danceable, and fun all at the same time. It is the kind of music that a wide range of people, no matter their social class, age, or race, can relate to. West says, "I rap in such a way where the hood can respect it; but I can sit right in front of a white executive and spit [perform] the exact same verse and he'll understand at least 80% of it. … People say you can't please everyone all the time. I don't believe it. I think I can."[3]

Powerful Words

One reason West's music is relevant is the lyrics. Many of his songs are autobiographical. They are rooted in everyday situations, such as working for minimum wage, going to college, and

While gangsta rappers portray a tough street life with their music, West is able to connect with his audience and rap about his insecurities.

loving family, which most people can relate to. West says, "Just think about whatever you've been through in the past week, and I have a song about that."[4]

His songs also reveal his insecurities, which was new to hip-hop music. Gangsta rappers portrayed themselves as tougher than their audience. West, on the other hand, connected with his audience by admitting his vulnerabilities. According to Brown,

> where gangsta rap had traditionally been about "hoods" and "sets" and keeping outsiders out, often times only allowing them access if they were music buyers, West flipped the script and sought to offer his fans unlimited access into his own insecurities as a star. In so doing, West was building a bond with his fans through accessibility few rap stars offered

before. He made his fans feel as though he wasn't above them, but rather just like them in a kinship few hip-hop stars had achieved.[5]

Besides dealing with his own personal issues, West's lyrics delve into social issues that concern him such as racism, materialism, and spousal abuse. Many young people share West's distress about social injustice, which connects them with the rapper. In addition, with his Grammy Award–winning hit "Jesus Walks," he brought religion to hip-hop music. Mixing the two was a daring move and also helped broaden rap music's audience.

Differences Musically

Melodically West's music is also innovative. He has never been afraid to experiment and try new things. By mixing and speeding up live instrumentation, gospel choirs, old rhythm and blues, and soul samples with traditional rap beats, he created a new and different sound, which links the past to the future.

This pleases fans of all ages. Older people, who may not have been hip-hop enthusiasts before, recognize the soul samples in West's music and become fans. Younger people enjoy the fresh new sound while discovering classic rhythm and blues. "I feel like a lot of the soul that's in those old records that I sample is in me," West explains. "So when I hear them and I put them with the drums and I bring them to the new millennium."[6]

A New Look

Unlike gangsta rappers who traditionally dressed in baggy pants and oversize team jerseys, West has his own sense of style, which sets him apart. He often sports pastel polo shirts with the collar sticking up, sweater vests, sports jackets, khakis, and loafers. West's preppy style gave hip-hop music a gentler and more innocent look that pleased both young people and their parents. Like his words and beats, West's sense of style helped take hip-hop music into the mainstream.

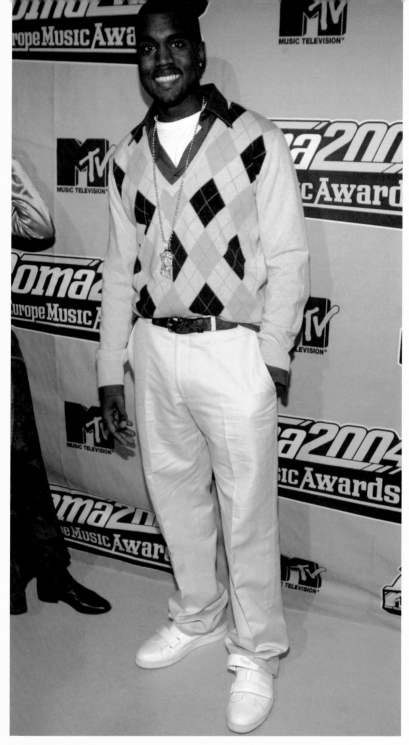

West's unique sense of "preppy" style sets him apart from others in the hip-hop industry.

A Fashionable Standout

Kanye West has always loved clothes and fashion. He has his own sense of style and likes to stand out in a crowd. According to the article, "Style Icon: Kanye West," on AskMen.com, he is known to wear "satin blazers, suits and crisp dress shirts paired with funky, futuristic-looking high-tops … polo shirts, cable-knit sweaters, fur, and '70s- and '80s-inspired sportswear."

The article also states, "West is not afraid of color. From lime green to pink, violet and electric blue, this musician frequently uses pops of bold color to liven up his distinctive look. His standby accessories include big, chunky gold necklaces and unusual eyewear."

West often calls himself the Louis Vuitton Don and favors apparel and leather goods by that designer.

AskMen.com, "Style Icon: Kanye West," AskMen.com, www.askmen.com/fashion/style_icon/14_style_icon.html.

Kanye West has never been afraid to be himself. He became a superstar on his own terms. In so doing, he changed the look and sound of hip-hop music and opened it up to a wider audience. According to writer Walt Mueller, "West has set himself apart from the crowd through his willingness to sacrifice convention for creativity. For many, his music is a breath of fresh air."[7]

Chapter 1

A Strong Influence

Kanye Omari West was born in Atlanta, Georgia, on June 8, 1977, to Ray and Donda West. Ray was one of the first black photojournalists to work for the *Atlanta Journal-Constitution* and Donda was a college professor with a doctorate degree in English. They were social activists who believed it was their personal responsibility to speak out and take action against social injustice. As a member of the Black Panthers, Ray fought against racial discrimination. Kanye's grandparents, too, had taken a strong stand against racism during the civil rights movement of the 1950s. In fact, Kanye's grandfather, Porty Williams, took part in a number of sit-ins and was arrested in one along with Kanye's mother who was six years old at the time. Kanye's family had a tremendous influence on him. It shaped him into a confident, socially aware, and outspoken person. In his song, "Never Let Me Down," West raps about his mother's arrest and how his family's social consciousness affected him.

A Special Name for a Special Child

Even before Kanye was born, his parents felt he would be special. Like many parents to be, they prayed for a healthy baby. They also prayed that their child would be brilliant. When it came to naming the baby, they wanted to give him a name that reflected their hopes for the child as well as his culture. Donda spent hours studying

West's parents were strong social activists. His father was a member of the Black Panthers, a black group that fought against racial discrimination.

The Black Panther Party

As a young man, Ray West was a member of the Black Panther Party. It was a militant organization founded by black activists Bobby Seale and Huey Newton in 1966. Its goal was to improve the lives of black people in America. To achieve this, the Black Panthers vowed to defend black Americans from any oppressors through any means necessary, including violent actions. The Black Panther Party is the only black organization in the history of the United States in which the members were armed.

The Black Panther Party developed a ten-point plan. In the plan it called for better housing, better jobs, a decent education, free health care, and more power for all black people, among other things. One of the things the Black Panthers did was set up a free breakfast program for poor children. The success of this program led the federal government to enact school breakfast programs.

In 1968 party leader Huey Newton was arrested for manslaughter. This caused the Black Panthers Party to start to fall apart. By the late 1970s it had disbanded.

African names. When she found the names Kanye and Omari, she knew she had found what she was looking for. *Kanye* is an Ethiopian name that means "the only one." *Omari* is a Swahili name that means "wise man." Those names were perfect for a special and brilliant child. Plus, his initials would be K.O., which is a boxing term that stands for a knockout. To Donda, those initials signified that her son would be tough and stand up for himself. "I knew he would be our only child, set apart, and special,"[8] she said.

Still a Family

Kanye was a happy and well-loved baby. Although his parents divorced when he was three years old, the pair remained friends

While West was growing up, he and his mother lived in Chicago as well as in various Chicago suburbs.

and made sure Kanye knew that their separation had nothing to do with him. After the divorce, his father moved to Maryland where he became a Christian counselor. Kanye and his mother moved to Illinois, where Donda took a job as an English professor at Chicago State University. While Kanye was growing up, they lived in Chicago as well as in various Chicago suburbs. Although Kanye was far away from his father and both sets of his grandparents, who lived in Delaware and Oklahoma, his mother made sure that he spent as much time as possible with them. He spent every summer with the Wests and visited his mother's family often.

The time Kanye spent with his father and his grandparents helped shape his character. As a photographer, Ray viewed the world through an artist's eyes. His father's influence helped Kanye to develop a unique perspective on the world around him. Moreover Kanye inherited his father's creativity and artistic talent.

Kanye started drawing when he was three years old. According to his mother,

> even then, his talent stood out. He drew things that kids who were twice his age couldn't draw. He drew people—real people, not stick people. I remember having a conversation with him about colors and how a banana is supposed to be yellow and an orange should be orange. But he rarely made things the "right" color, not unless he wanted to. He would make the banana purple and the orange blue. I didn't tell him he was wrong.... He knew that a banana was actually yellow, but he wanted to make it purple and I didn't argue with him.... Kanye had a distinctive perspective. He always had his own spin on things.[9]

By watching and listening to his father, Kanye also became socially aware. Both his parents encouraged the boy to speak out against injustice and be unafraid to express the truth as he saw it. In the future, he would often be called arrogant because he spoke out, especially when he spoke out about what he perceived as injustices against himself. He was doing what he had been raised to do—expressing his personal truths.

Ray's parents also had a big impact on Kanye. They were devout Christians. During his visits, they took their grandson to church and worked hard to instill Christian values in him. When Kanye was in Chicago, he and Donda attended church regularly and Kanye went to Sunday school. "I was really raised in the church, and raised as a good Black man," West told *Ebony* magazine reporter, Kimberly Davis. "I don't want to offend people. I want to help people and do as much as I can for them. And I think God blesses me in return."[10]

The Williams' Influence

Kanye and his mother visited her family in Oklahoma often, too. They also had a big influence on Kanye. His grandfather, Portwood "Buddy" Williams, was a huge fan of professional boxer Mohammad Ali. Ali was known for boasting about himself.

But he backed up his bragging with strength and talent. Kanye's grandfather shared his passion for Ali with his grandson and encouraged him to exhibit the same kind of bold self-confidence as the boxer. Kanye took his grandfather's words to heart. In the future, he would become known for his self-confidence, which he attributes to Buddy. He mentions this in his song "Roses."

Kanye also got his determination and solid work ethic from his grandfather. Buddy worked at many jobs. Although some were difficult and demeaning, he never quit. As a young man, he worked at a train station shining shoes. On several occasions his passersby spit on him and demeaned him with racial slurs. Buddy wanted to quit, but he did not. He was determined to provide for his family. So he swallowed his anger and pride and said nothing. Working was more important than his ego. Eventually he became a successful businessman. The example he set had a lasting influence on Kanye. Like his grandfather, Kanye showed great determination when he refused to give up on his dream of becoming a rapper despite many rejections and disappointments. And, like his grandfather, his work ethic shines. As a music producer, Kanye is known to spend long hours in the studio.

The Williams family also contributed to Kanye's interest in music. Kanye's Aunt Shirlie and Aunt Klaye were the first black children in Oklahoma City to appear on television. Shirlie played the piano and Klaye sang. The two went on to perform all over the United States. As adults, Shirlie directed many church choirs and Klaye became a professional jazz singer.

Kanye had many positive role models. In 2007 his mother said, "when I watch Kanye today, I see in him the courage of my dad and the strength of my mother, the diligence of his father's dad and the devoutedness of his father's mother. I see the creativity of his dad, Ray West, and my sensitivity. Kanye embodies aspects of the entire West and Williams families."[11]

Mama's Boy

Although all of his family members played a role in molding Kanye's character, his mother influenced him the most. For the most part, Kanye grew up as the only child of a single mother, and

West grew up an only child of a single mother, Donda. Although Donda had a full-time job she was devoted to her son and his interests.

the two were extremely close. Despite holding down a full-time job at Chicago State University and often working one or two other jobs in order to make ends meet, Donda was very involved in her son's life. She volunteered in his school and spent almost all of her free time with him. Every Saturday she took him to the Chicago Academy of Arts for free art lessons. After the lessons, the two toured Chicago. They went to museums and libraries and visited historical buildings. Donda thought it was important to nurture her son's talents and to take him to places where he could learn about and experience the world. They also took vacation trips to place like Washington, D.C., and Disney World.

For much of Kanye's life, he and his mom were inseparable. Donda was his greatest supporter and cheerleader. Years later Kanye said,

> After my parents got divorced and we moved to Chicago at age 3, I would go visit my father on Christmas, during breaks, and the summer. But the rest of that time, my mother was my everything.... I love her. She is my best friend in the whole world. My mother let me work on my music, she helped me out, she used to drive me to the studio. She was really my first manager.... Even me sitting back and thinking about all the stuff now, thinking about all the stuff my mother has done for me, it makes me wanna call her.[12]

While working hard not to stifle his creativity or break his spirit, Donda set boundaries for Kanye and expected him to stay within them. She had high expectations for him. She insisted he be honest, polite, loving, respectful, and hard working. At the same time, she wanted him to be his own person. She encouraged Kanye to be outspoken. She did not want him to conform to society's rules if he thought those rules were unjust. For example, although she expected Kanye to be polite to adults, she also wanted him to question authority and be aware that not everything adults did or said was correct.

For the most part, Kanye was a good child. He tried to please his mother and usually did what was expected of him. In return she rewarded him by giving him almost everything he wanted. Although Donda often seemed to be permissive with Kanye, on those occasions when he acted inappropriately, she punished him in her own unique way. For instance, when Kanye was a teenager, Donda caught him watching an X-rated video. As punishment, she made him write a research paper on the impact that watching X-rated movies has on teenagers. Until the paper was completed to his mother's satisfaction, Kanye was grounded.

Even when she disciplined Kanye, Donda made sure to let him know how special he was and how much she loved him. She worked hard to teach her child to love himself. She felt that this was the best way to ensure he would grow up to be a strong well-adjusted person with the confidence to achieve his dreams. Kanye took all his mother's lessons to heart. Today his self-confidence is one of his trademarks.

Donda's guidance, love, and support had such a huge impact on Kanye that he wrote a song titled, "Hey Mama," to honor her. In it, he explains that Donda is not only his mother but also his dear friend. He talks about how hard she worked to care for and how much he loves and respects her for it.

Standing Out

Maybe because his family made him feel special or because his mother worked hard to encourage his creative side, Kanye always wanted to stand out and be different. Even as a young child, he insisted on doing things his own way. In order to gain admission to Vanderpoel Elementary Magnet School, a public school for the arts, Kanye had to take a series of tests. In one test, he was asked to draw a picture of a man. Kanye wanted to draw a picture of a football player instead. The test administrator explained that all the other children had drawn a picture of a man. Kanye did not want his picture to be like all the others. He drew a picture of a football player. The picture, he explained to the test administrator, was of a man who just happened to be wearing a football uniform.

Kanye was admitted to Vanderpoel, which he attended from kindergarten through eighth grade. He managed to stand out throughout his school career. He won many art contests and developed an early interest in fashion design. This was unusual for a little boy, but he loved color and style and was not afraid to be different.

West signs copies of his CD Graduation in New York City. He describes himself as a creative person, and oversees the design of all CD artwork.

He liked the fact that his interest in fashion design set him apart from his peers. Interestingly, he has his own fashion line today, and he oversees the designs all his videos and the artwork on his CDs. He thinks of his work in music as designing too. "I have to be creative at all times and I have to learn. I don't know any other way. I'm a designer, and rap is just one of my designs,"[13] he says.

Kanye also stood out musically. In third grade he became interested in rap music. At home he would stand in front of a mirror and practice rapping. At school he entered the annual talent shows, which he always won. He was so good that he helped the other contestants sharpen their acts because he knew he would win anyway. Many of the teachers at Vanderpoel took to calling the talent shows, "The Kanye West Show," because he was always the star.

Celebrity Status

Kanye had a chance to really stand out when he was ten years old. His mother was offered a position teaching English in Nanjing, China. The two moved there for a year. Most of the

What Is Hip-Hop?

On the Web site, Davey D's Hip Hop Corner, hip-hop historian Davey D defines hip-hop as "an art form that includes deejaying (cuttin' & scratchin'), emceeing/rappin', break dancing, and grafiti art."

He explains that break dancing is "a colorful and acrobatic form of dance, which includes headspins, backspins. . . . [It] traces its roots to the form of African martial arts known as capoeta. This form of fighting was employed by revolting slaves who were brought to Brazil."

Davey D says rapping involves "saying rhymes to the beat of music, [it] was originally called emceeing. It draws its roots from the Jamaican art form known as toasting."

Deejaying, he explains, "is the manipulation of a record over a particular groove so it produces strange sounds. This was invented either by Grand Master Flash or Grand Master Theodore, two popular disc jockeys from the Bronx."

Davey D's Hip Hop Corner, "What Is Hip Hop?" http://www.daveyd.com/whatishipdav.html.

people in Nanjing had never seen a black child in person. Kanye stood out without trying. People stared at him wherever he went. They crowded around him and begged for a chance to touch him. Because they had seen African Americans break-dancing in movies and television, they begged Kanye to break-dance.

Some children would have been embarrassed by this sort of attention. Kanye, however, loved it and used it to his advantage. He taught himself to break-dance and then danced on the street for his Chinese fans. They threw coins at him, which he used to buy edible treats. "I think," Kanye says, "that got me ready to be a celeb because, at the time, a lot of Chinese had never seen a black person. They would come up and stare at me, rub my skin."[14]

Kanye also stood out from the other foreign children in Nanjing because he learned to speak Chinese. It is possible that his musical ear helped him to pick up the language, which has four tones and inflections. Because he was fluent in the language, he served as his mother's translator. The two took full advantage of their time in China. Kanye took tai chi and art lessons, and the pair traveled throughout Asia. It was a wonderful experience that holds a special place in Kanye's memory.

Finding His Passion

A few years after returning from China, Kanye developed an interest in designing video games. At first, his primary interest was in designing the characters and scenery. Once he got involved

At age 13, West had dreams of getting a recording contract and becoming more popular than the young rap group Kriss Kross.

with creating the sound and background music, he lost interest in the artwork. He was fascinated with producing music. This new interest led him back to his early interest in rap. Soon he was creating his own beats and lyrics. When he was twelve years old, he wrote his first complete song, "Green Eggs and Ham." He convinced his mother to pay twenty-five dollars so he could record it.

Little did Donda know that "Green Eggs and Ham" would be just the beginning. She expected her son to go to college, earn multiple degrees, and then pursue a career in art. Kanye, on the other hand, was already thinking about a future in music. He started selling beats to his friends and sent copies of his work to record companies. "I thought I was going to get signed back when I was 13 years old and come out with a record and take Kriss Kross [a 1990s rap group made up of young people] out,"[15] he recalls.

It took many years for Kanye to get signed to a recording contract. But that did not stop him from pursuing his dream. He had found his passion.

Chapter 2

Following His Dream

By the time Kanye West became a teenager, he had given up designing video games to focus on music. He had a vision of himself as a successful rapper and worked hard to turn his vision into reality.

Making Music

When West was fourteen, he got his first keyboard. He saved up his allowance to buy it, and his ever-supportive mother helped too. By working odd jobs, he earned enough money over the next few years to buy a music sampler, an electronic device used to manipulate sound on a computer; a mixing board, a tool to balance sound; a turntable; and a drum machine. He spent almost all his free time in his bedroom experimenting with the equipment. According to his mother,

> Kanye dreamed of doing music from the time he was very young. I first noticed it when he was in third grade. That and drawing were his passions. But somewhere along the way music took over. Kanye spent hours and hours, mixing, rapping, and writing. It was nonstop. He became so involved that his socializing revolved around that studio in his room. When his grandparents Chick and Buddy would visit, Kanye would come out of his room only to eat and go to the bathroom.

COMMON *was the first rapper to be signed to West's*
G.O.O.D. *label, and the two remain close friends.*

He was amazingly focused. If anyone, including dad, wanted
to spend time with Kanye, they'd have to go to his room and
get in a few words while Kanye made music.[16]

Even West's social life revolved around music. His friends were
other young rappers. Among them were COMMON, Mikkey,

Rhymefest, Gravity, and GLC. West still remains in close contact with these men today. COMMON was the first person West signed to his Getting Out Our Dreams (G.O.O.D. Music) record label, and he made a guest appearance on Mikkey's 2008 CD. "We have always helped each other, that's how it goes. There was a whole circle of us back then, such as Kanye, Rhymefest, GLC, and me," Mikkey recalls. "We would all work on songs together, come up with patterns or lines, help each other overall. Sometimes, we'll call each other on the phone and we'll tell each other which lines we like, or if the chorus should be reworked, things like that."[17]

Soon, West was selling his beats to his friends for fifty dollars a tune. He used the money he earned to buy more equipment. At night, West and his friends often snuck out to hip-hop clubs. Although West was underage and used fake identification to get into the clubs, he was not interested in drinking or getting into trouble. All he wanted to do was listen to the music.

Eager to Learn

Donda secretly followed her son to the clubs in order to make sure he was safe. Although her concern for him and her support for his music might have seemed extreme, it helped West to meet legendary hip-hop producer No I.D.

Donda met No I.D.'s mother at Chicago State University. She asked her if No I.D. would help West with his music. At the time, West was only fourteen years old. No I.D. was six years older than West. He was already an established hip-hop producer. At first No I.D. was unenthusiastic about helping the younger boy. But West was so eager to learn and caught on so quickly that No I.D. soon changed his mind.

No I.D. taught West everything he knew about music production, including the best way to sample music. He also introduced him to the idea of incorporating excerpts from old rhythm and blues tunes in his beats. No I.D.'s teaching, combined with the hours West spent experimenting and practicing, really helped

No I.D.

Kanye West's mentor, No I.D., was one of the most success-ful hip-hop and rhythm-and-blues producers in Chicago during the late 1990s. He was known as the Godfather of Chicago Hip-Hop.

Born in Chicago as Dion Wilson, No I.D. has also been known as Ernest Wilson and Immenslope. Besides being a producer, No I.D. is also a performer. He released his first album *Accept Your Own and Be Yourself* in 1997. His second album was a two-album set called *The Sampler*.

No I.D. is best known for his work producing music for his lifelong friend, COMMON. He has also produced songs for DMX, Toni Braxton, G-Unit, Lauren Hill, Bow-wow, Jermaine Dupri, Alicia Keys, Jay-Z, Rhymefest, and Killer Mike, among others. His work is featured on West's 2008 release *808s & Heartbreak*.

West to improve as a producer. Years later, West would refer to No I.D. as his mentor in his songs "Big Brother," and "Last Call." No I.D. explains,

> the mentor part really came from him being a shorty with no father and me knowing him and helping him with every aspect of life, not just music.... I did show him all the music stuff but he got a lot of stuff from other people too.... He was just one of them energetic kids—teach me everything, teach me anything.... He always evolved.... He always working to achieve something new everyday.... It feels good to see the level that Kanye's ... at because we all started in basements like as kids with nobody, no help, no hook-up, no special connections.... For us all to reach out here and touch the world and do what we are doing, you got to love it.[18]

Getting an Education

When West was not in his studio working on his music, he attended Polaris High School, a public high school in Oak Lawn, Illinois, a suburb of Chicago where he and his mother lived. He was a good student who took extra music and art classes and won a number of art contests.

In 1995 at seventeen years of age, he graduated from high school. He was offered a scholarship to study fine art at the prestigious American Academy of Art in Chicago. This was an honor. At his mother's urging, West attended the academy. But he left after only one semester. Although he did well and had

West returned to Chicago State University in 2005 as surprise professor to a group of music students. He dropped out of the university in his third semester to focus on his music.

an impressive portfolio, West did not want to pursue a career in art. Hip-hop music was his first love. He wanted to make it his life's work.

His mother supported him in his desire to become a music producer and rapper, but she wanted him to get a postsecondary education first. To please her, West enrolled in Chicago State University where his mother was now the head of the English Department. From the start, he was unenthusiastic. He became an English major because he thought it would help him to write his raps and because his mother could register him for English classes. This kept him from waiting in line like the other students.

He showed little interest in his classes and frequently missed them, opting to stay home and work on his music instead. When he was on campus, he spent most of his time hanging around the music studios experimenting with the equipment.

In an effort to keep him in school, his mother had a friend, who was also a professor, talk to West. Donda's friend realized that the young man's heart was not in his studies. He had other plans for his life and was committed to succeeding as a musician. She saw how serious West was about his music and tried to convince Donda that West did not have to complete college, at least not at that time, to succeed in life. Although Donda understood and even agreed theoretically, it was hard for her to admit that West's path lay in a different direction than the one she envisioned for him.

College Dropout

As much as West wanted to please his mother, he knew that he could not succeed in college and dedicate himself to his music at the same time. So, at nineteen years old in his third semester of college, West dropped out. He explains why:

> College is not particularly everybody's answer. Sometimes it might be better for someone to go to a trade school. [People] try to make it seem like if you go to college and you get all A's, that you'll move to the suburbs, have

The Language of Hip-Hop

Hip-hop has a language all its own. Here are a few hip-hop terms and their meanings:

A-level artist: A top selling artist.

A&R (artist and repertoire): A record company executive who finds new talent.

b-boy: Someone who break-dances.

bite: To copy someone else's lyrics.

bling bling: Jewelry.

cheese : Money.

crew: A group or band.

crib: Home.

deejay: Individual who manipulates records.

def: Excellent.

dis: To insult.

emcee (MC): A rap performer.

freestyle: Improvising lyrics during a performance.

front: To pretend to be something or someone.

rap: A form of poetry, which focuses more on rhythm than traditional poetry.

rewire: To remake previously recorded music.

sample: An excerpt of a previously recorded song.

school: A specific era in hip-hop history, as in old or new school.

screw: To play beats at a slow speed.

slamming: Good, attractive dynamic.

spit: To recite rap lyrics.

tag: To create graffiti.

Trump: To be rich.

yo: you, your

2.5 kids and live happily ever after. But in many cases life just doesn't work like that. There are lots of careers that don't involve college. What I'm saying is, make your own decisions.[19]

Even though West made his own decision, he did not want to upset his mother. Plus, he was a little afraid of how she would react to his plan. In his song "Graduation Day," he talks about his decision, how he knows his mother will disapprove of it, how he does not want to disappoint her, and how he hopes she will understand that he has to follow his dream.

So he did not drop out of college without talking to Donda first. He told her his reasons for wanting to drop out and tried to make her understand. It was not easy, but Donda had always urged her son not to conform and to follow his heart. She realized that this was exactly what he was doing and agreed to West's plan. "It was drummed into my head that college was the ticket to a good life, but some career goals don't require college," she explained years later. "For Kanye ... it was more about having the guts to embrace who you are, rather than following the path society has carved out for you."[20]

Donda gave West one year to make it in the music business. At the end of the year, if he was not able to support himself making music he promised to go back to college. In addition, since West was no longer a student, his mother expected him to pay her two hundred dollars a month for his room and board. She wanted him to see what it was like to support himself and to learn financial responsibility.

Earning a Living

In order to earn enough money to pay his mother for room and board and to buy gas for the new car his father had bought him, West took a job as a telemarketer. He was always a smooth talker and quite charming. He made lots of sales and even got some bonus checks. He also worked as a sales clerk at Gap. In the future he would write about that experience in his song "Spaceship."

After getting home from work as a sales clerk at the Gap, West would work on beats for artists such as Lil' Kim.

When he got home from work, he spent most of his time creating beats for other artists, including Lil Kim, the Madd Rapper, and Trina and Tamara. This left little time for his own music.

West often stayed up all night just so he could work on his own tunes. West explains,

> I was still making ends meet by … doing beats. I used to charge people $250 to $500 per beat. I made a way just to hustle. You know hustling doesn't mean "Ah, you just sell drugs." … [It means] hustling any way you can to maintain a lifestyle and then also, in your spare time, chase your dreams. So whenever I would finish work, I would be up until 4:00 in the morning … focusing on my dream and praying for the day where I could just do that all the time.[21]

Although West's dream was to perform, it was his work as a music producer that was proving he could make music his career. West came up with the idea of mixing samples of old soul tunes with speeded up vocals and live instrumentation. The sound he created was fresh and new. Lots of people took notice. When Gravity, a rapper West was working with, got a record deal, he bought a beat from West for eight thousand dollars. This was enough to prove to Donda that West could earn a living as a musician. It was at this point that both she and West realized that he would not be going back to college any time soon.

Bigger than Jermaine Dupri

Once it became apparent that West would indeed be able to make a living with his music, his mother urged him to get his own apartment. As much as she loved having him around, the constant coming and going of West's clients at all hours of the night combined with the sound tracks that played all the time were hard for her to handle. Although all the rappers were always polite to Donda and she liked the music, she had had enough. She missed her peace and quiet and her privacy.

By the time West was twenty years old, he had become a well-known music producer in Chicago. Among his clients were established rappers, like Mase and Jermaine Dupri. Yet West was not satisfied. Although he enjoyed working behind the scenes

West bragged to Columbia Records executive Michael Mauldin (L) saying he was going to be bigger than Jermaine Dupri (R) not knowing that Dupri was his son.

creating tracks for other artists, his dream was to write, produce, and perform his own music. When Columbia Records showed an interest in signing him, West thought his dream was about to come true. The record company sent a limousine to pick him up. This was standard procedure, but West did not know it. He thought they sent the limousine because they were so impressed with him. West felt extremely important. He was so confident that Columbia wanted him and that he would be a big star that he boasted to Columbia's executive officer Michael Mauldin that he was more talented and would be more successful than Michael Jackson or Jermaine Dupri. West did not know that Mauldin was Dupri's father. Mauldin did not appreciate West's comment and decided not to sign him after all.

This was the first, but not the last, time that West's dream of becoming a performer would be shot down. Although he was disheartened by the rejection, West did not let this rejection or those that followed destroy his dream. Instead he worked harder, both as a producer and on his own music believing that eventually he would succeed. His mother explains,

> He was producing music and writing raps like the world was coming to an end . But no matter how great his music was, no one wanted to give him a deal. He would soon learn that it would take more than talent, good looks, and desire to land a deal. He would have to add resilience to the mix. If you're going to crumble when you hear the word "no", you can forget about making it in the entertainment business. You have to develop tough skin. If they kick you down and bruise that ego, you have to brush yourself off and get right back up. And that's just what Kanye did.[22]

Leaving Chicago

Just as West's mother found the constant traffic going in and out of her son's studio disturbing, so did West's landlord. He threatened to evict the young man from his apartment if the continuous flow of people did not stop. Threatened with eviction and rejected by Columbia Records, West decided it was time to leave Chicago.

West knew that in order to make it big in the rap industry he needed to go to New York, where the hip-hop scene was much bigger.

Although West was already a successful producer, Chicago's hip-hop scene was quite small. Hip-hop's biggest stars and most successful record companies were located in New York and California. West reasoned that if he was going to make it big as a rap star, he needed to go to New York in order to meet and work with people who could help his career.

Deciding to leave Chicago was a difficult decision for West. He was only twenty three years-old at the time and had spent most of his life in the Chicago area. He had many friends in the hip-hop community there, and he had made a name for himself. In Chicago he was a big fish in a small pond. In New York he would be just the opposite. Leaving his mother was also hard. The two had never been separated for any length of time, and he depended on her for help and support. Although Donda hated to see him go, she knew it was the right move. Through a friend who lived in the New York metropolitan area, she found West an apartment in Newark, New Jersey. He took it sight unseen.

In 2001 West and his mother loaded his belongings into a rental truck, which the two drove to Newark. West loved his new apartment. It had a living room with a glass ceiling. Looking up at the sky during the day and at the stars at night inspired him. He believed he would create great music here. Surely a record company would recognize his talent as a rapper and sign him. He planned to do whatever it took to make that happen.

Chapter 3

More Than a Producer

As soon as West got settled in his new home, he made a demo tape of his beats and took it to all the major hip-hop record labels in the New York area. He hoped that his skill as a beat maker would help him to get his foot in the door of the New York record industry and eventually get him signed as a rapper.

Meeting Jay-Z

West's demo tape was not met with enthusiasm. Although he was well-known in Chicago, he was not in New York. Many of the record company executives who he hoped would listen to his tape did not bother to play it. Kyambo "Hip-Hop" Joshua of Roc-A-Fella Records, however, did listen to it. As the A&R (artist and repertoire) man at Roc-A-Fella, his job was to seek out new talent. He was impressed with West's unique way of blending samples of old rhythm and blues and soul classics with modern beats and sped up the vocals.

He invited the young man to a recording session in which Jay-Z would be recording tracks for his upcoming album, *The Blueprint*. Besides being one of hip-hop's biggest stars, Jay-Z was one of the owners of Roc-A-Fella Records.

West was nervous at the thought of meeting Jay-Z. But he did not show it. His belief in his own talent helped calm him. "I was definitely intimidated because Jay-Z is a superstar, and

Jay-Z

Shawn Carter, who is better known as Jay-Z, is one of the most successful rappers and businessmen in hip-hop today. He grew up poor in Brooklyn, New York, where he developed his interest in music at a young age.

Because he could not get a recording contract, he and his friends, Damon Dash and Kareem Biggs, started Roc-A-Fella Records. He released his first album, *Reasonable Doubt* in 1996 and won his first Grammy Award in 1999 for his album *Vol. 2 Hard Knock Life*. He has since gone on to win many awards. In 2006 he was named Greatest Emcee of All Time by MTV.

Jay-Z has also met with great success as a businessman. He has been the chief executive officer of both Roc-A-Fella Records and Def Jam Recordings. He co-owns the New Jersey Nets basketball team. At the close of 2008, he had sold more than 26 million records in the United States. He married singer and actress Beyoncé Knowles in April 2008.

one of my idols. But even if he told me one of my beats stinks, it wouldn't have crushed me. I still got real high self-esteem,"[23] he recalls.

Jay-Z loved West's beats. He used five of them on his album. Most notably, West provided the tracks for "Takeover" and "Izzo (H.O.V.A.)." "Takeover" features samples of the Doors' song, "Five to One," while "Izzo (H.O.V.A.)" features samples of the Jackson 5's song, "I Want You Back."

West's work on *The Blueprint* helped to make the album a hit. And his association with Jay-Z and Roc-A-Fella Records gave him the credentials he needed to succeed in New York. "That was the turning point of my life," West explains. "Jay made all the difference. I can't say that I wouldn't have done it without him, but he made it easier because he gave me a stamp, he gave me the streets. The Roc-A-Fella chain helped me get my name."[24]

West considers working with Jay-Z a turning-point in his life, and even wrote a song titled "Big Brother" about him.

West continued working with Jay-Z and learned a lot from him. His relationship with Jay-Z was so important to his career that he wrote the song, "Big Brother," about it. In the song he calls Jay-Z his big brother and thanks the older rapper for all he has done for him.

The Hottest Producer

West's work with Jay-Z gave him the name recognition he lacked when he arrived in New York. The hip-hop community was impressed with his creativity and skill as a producer, as well as his solid work ethic and attention to detail. Word quickly spread about how he spent hours working on every track. For West it was not enough for his clients to be satisfied with his work; he had to be satisfied too. "Every single song he makes," Jay-Z explains, "he makes because he thinks it's the best record at that specific time. He may not think it next week, but that week, he thought it was the best record he could make."[25]

It was not long before West was the most in-demand music producer around. Between 2002 and 2003, he produced tracks for such stars as Alicia Keyes, Cam'ron, Scarface, Jamie Foxx, Jay-Z, Beanie Sigel, Beyoncé, Ludacris, Janet Jackson, Talib Kweli, and Twista. He did not forget his longtime friend, COMMON, and continued to make beats for him as well. His work made an impression on performers, critics, industry executives, and the public. MTV reporter Shaheem Reid explains,

> The first record that really brought Kanye West to my attention was Beanie Sigel's "The Truth" … I had no idea that the producer of the song would grow to be a superstar. Then Kanye hit me with the whammy on Jay-Z's *Dynasty* album: "This Can't Be Life." Incredible. My favorite song off the album and one of the best album cuts you'll ever hear. The soulful loop was drenched with so much pain and hope…. Then I started to research Kanye. "He's gonna be one of the best producers in the game," I thought. "He confirmed my suspicions on Beanie's "Nothing Like It" from *The Reason* album…. His music sounded like the civil-rights movement mixed with backwoods juke joints and Sunday morning church services…. Even back then Kanye could hit you with so many emotions in his tracks."[26]

A Performer Too

Even though West was busy producing tracks for other artists, it did not stop him from pursuing his dream of being a performer. He told every record company executive and every artist he worked with that he was also a rapper and rapped for them

West is known for spending hours in the recording studio getting his tracks "just right."

every chance he got. He was convinced that someday he would be a superstar.

The rest of the hip-hop community did not share West's conviction. More often than not, when he talked about his ability to perform, he was ignored, and when he did rap, his raps were met with uncomfortable silence. There were a number of reasons why he was not taken seriously. First, he was a producer. Generally hip-hop producers stay behind the scenes. According to West, "people have all these stereotypes. People use to say white people couldn't rap before Eminem. They also said producers can't rap. That's before I come out. I don't know if people ever thought about the fact that Prince made his own beats, that Stevie Wonder made his own albums."[27]

Second, West was different from the gangsta rappers who were popular at the time. He had never hustled on the street and did not pretend he had. Nor, did he try to change his appearance or his persona to suit the gangsta image. Because he was not the stereotypical rapper, record company executives did not think he had commercial potential. The idea that someone like him could be a rap star was considered ridiculous. Even Jay-Z was disdainful. In an article in *Time* magazine, writer Josh Tyrangiel talks to Jay-Z and Damon Dash, former chief executive officer of Roc-A-Fella Records, about West. "Kanye wore a pink shirt with the collar sticking up and Gucci loafers. It was obvious we were not from the same place or cut from the same cloth," Dash explains. "We all grew up street guys who had to do whatever we had to do to get by," Jay-Z adds. "Then there's Kanye, who to my knowledge has never hustled a day in his life. I didn't see how it could work."[28]

If West had tried to present himself differently, he might have met with more success. There were gangsta rappers who were not as tough or as streetwise as they pretended to be. West refused to change or lie about who he was. He believed in himself and was confident his talent would speak for itself. Despite the fact that he had never hustled on the streets, he felt that his persistence in the face of criticism proved he was just as tough as his peers. He explains,

> It was a strike against me that I didn't wear baggy jeans and jerseys and that I never hustled, never sold drugs. But for me to have the opportunity to stand in front of a bunch of executives and present myself, I had to hustle in my own way. I can't tell you how frustrating it was that they didn't get that. No joke—I'd leave meetings crying all the time.[29]

Signed

West continued to struggle to be taken seriously as a rapper. Despite being ignored and rejected, he rapped whenever he was around record company executives and hip-hop celebrities in hopes that someone would appreciate his talent. "It was hard coming in," he recalls. "That struggle to get through the gate and everybody's dissing [insulting] you. A&R people saying, 'You're never going to make it! No one's ever going to play this track!' People talk to you the way guards talk to prisoners."[30]

When Damon Dash of Roc-a-Fella Records thought West was going to sign with Capitol, he got worried and offered West a deal.

He was especially disappointed when he was ignored by Jay-Z who had a concert in New York's Madison Square Garden. Jay-Z invited a number of different rappers to join him onstage. In spite of the fact that he was performing some of West's beats, Jay-Z did not include West. West was not even given a backstage pass to the event.

And when Roc-A-Fella's Roc the Mic tour went to Chicago, West thought he would be invited to perform. After all, Chicago was his hometown, and a number of his beats were to be included in the show. On this occasion, he was backstage waiting to come out to sing a verse of "We are the Champions." But the music switched to something else when he was about to make his entrance. According to his mother,

> it was no coincidence. It was just a blunt way of saying, "Not this time dude." Kanye was pretty down about it. But feeling down and letting people get you down are two different things. Kanye was on a mission and nothing or no one could stop him. Had he been another type of person, one who'd march to the beat of someone else's drum or one who listened to the naysayers he might have left the rap game.[31]

To prove his ability, he performed "Jesus Walks," a song that was to become one of his most successful creations, for a number of record company executives. One executive offered to buy the song from West for a gospel singer to record. West refused to sell it. West wanted to record it, and his other tunes, himself. But no one was interested in signing him. He was too different. And he was such a gifted producer that the record companies were reluctant to use him for anything else.

Finally in 2002 West got the ear of Capitol Record's A&R man, Joe "3H" Weinberger. Weinberger was amazed by West's talent. He recalls,

> Kanye was never down on himself. He'd be ready to rap on the spot, ready to tell his story on the spot, ready to make a record on the spot. He was probably the hungriest

dude I ever saw. Whatever it takes. He wasn't all caked up [boastful] yet, but he still had his Kanye swagger. It was definite star quality the day I saw him. He played me three songs and I was like, "What!?" His flow was different, his beats were great, he was performing the whole time. The energy was there, it was some real star-quality stuff.[32]

Weinberger worked hard to persuade the executives at Capitol to offer West a recording contract. It looked like they had a deal. But on the day the contract was to be signed, Capitol canceled. The executives decided that West was unmarketable. Once again West was rejected.

When Damon Dash and Jay-Z heard West was planning to sign with Capitol, they got worried. They were not convinced that West could succeed as a rapper, but they did not want to lose him as a producer. Up until that point, West had not been working for any one particular record company. He worked for different artists, many of whom were associated with Roc-A-Fella. If he signed with Capitol as a recording artist, however, he would also become Capitol's in-house producer. This meant he would no longer be able to work for artists associated with Roc-A-Fella.

Out of desperation, Roc-A-Fella offered to sign West too. "Honestly, everybody was just trying to figure out how to keep him around, because he was making these fantastic tracks. That's really how his record deal happened. We were like, 'OK, let's just give him a deal,'"[33] explains Jay-Z. Because West had agreed to sign with Capitol first, he turned Roc-A-Fella down. But when the Capitol deal fell through, he took Roc-A-Fella up on its offer.

A Terrible Accident

Although West now had a recording contract, his production schedule had not eased. If anything, it was even more hectic than before. In order to find time to work on his own material, he worked late at night. On October 23, 2003, he was driving back to his hotel from a recording session in Los Angeles. He was so exhausted that he fell asleep at the wheel, causing a near-fatal accident. Because his airbag did not deploy, his face smashed into the steering wheel. His jaw was broken in three places, his nose was crushed, and his ribs were fractured. So much blood and mucus filled his throat that he could hardly breathe, which could have killed him. Rescue workers used the Jaws of Life to free West from the mangled vehicle.

West spent eight hours in the emergency room before being sedated. He then spent four hours in surgery. He was in terrible pain throughout the ordeal. As soon as she heard, his mother rushed to his side. When she saw her son's swollen and battered face, which was three times its normal size, she did not recognize him.

The doctors wired West's jaw partly shut. They planned to remove the wires after six weeks. But because there was a problem, once the bones set, they had to break West's jaw all over again and rewire it closed. His injuries were so severe that it was doubtful that he would ever be able to talk normally again, let alone rap. He was lucky to be alive and he knew it. "I have flashbacks of what happened every day," he explains. "And anytime I hear about an accident my heart sinks in and I thank God I am still here. I found out how short life is and how blessed you are to be here."[34]

"Through the Wire"

West's accident could have ended his career as a rapper before it began. With his mouth was wired shut, he could barely speak. And he continued to be in pain for a long time. Many people would have given up. West, on the other hand, was inspired to use the accident for an autobiographical song called "Through the Wire," which he started composing as a way take his mind off his pain. He even had a drum machine sent to his hospital room so he could work on the beat.

West sampled Chaka Khan's "Through the Fire" to make his hit "Through the Wire" in which he raps through a wired jaw because of his near-fatal car accident.

Despite the doctors saying that it was impossible, West went into the studio to record the song just three weeks after the accident. Rappers often say that they "spit" their lyrics. With his jaw wired shut, West quite literally did spit the song through the wires in his mouth. He forced himself to get out the words clearly enough to be understood. This took tremendous mental and physical effort on his part.

As always, West was not satisfied until he thought the song was perfect. Featuring samples of Chaka Khan's "Through the Fire," the song was both heartbreaking and funny. It revealed a lot about West. In it he talks about the accident, being close to death, and how fortunate he was to survive. At the same time, he jokes about his liquid diet and the damage to his face, while explaining that although he may be down, he is not going to quit. West believed that by writing and recording, "Through the Wire" he would turn adversity into success. Whether or not he was right, remained to be seen.

Chapter 4

Superstar

Kanye West hoped that "Through the Wire" would convince the world that he was as tough as any gangsta rapper and as talented an emcee as he was a producer. Roc-A-Fella Records was skeptical. It did not want to put too much money into "Through the Wire." So West used his own money to make a music video. This was financially risky. If the song was a hit, West would recoup what he spent. If it failed, he would lose a large sum of money. Always confident, he believed "Through the Wire" would be a success.

West worked hard to make sure he was right. With his jaw still wired shut, he personally delivered the video to MTV and BET (Black Entertainment Television). He refused to leave either network until he was assured that the video would get air play. He also gave many interviews in an effort to publicize the song, even though it was physically painful for him to do so.

His efforts paid off. "Through the Wire" was a big hit, and the video won the 2004 Video of the Year Award at the 2004 Hip-Hop Music Awards. Its popularity convinced Roc-A-Fella Records to throw its full support behind West as he worked on his debut album, *College Dropout*.

A Chart-Topping Debut

While West was working on *College Dropout*, he continued producing tracks for other artists. He was responsible for such smash hits as Alicia Keys' "You Don't Know My Name," Jay-Z's

West won Video of the Year Award for "Through the Wire" at the 4th Annual BET Hip-Hop Music Awards.

"03 Bonnie & Clyde," and Ludicris's "Stand Up." Sometimes he worked on two or three recording sessions in a day, earning up to a hundred thousand dollars per track. He also managed to record "Slow Jamz," in collaboration with Twista and Jamie Foxx. It became a hit single. With "Through the Wire" topping the charts, too, West had two simultaneous hit songs.

Because West was so busy, it was difficult for him to complete his own album. His perfectionism, which caused him to keep redoing tracks, and the fact that he had medical appointments for his mouth and teeth added to the delays. It took him almost two years to record *College Dropout*. West wrote, produced, rapped, and sang for the album. He also designed the album cover and produced all the videos connected with it.

College Dropout hit the market in February 2004. In its first week, it sold 441,000 copies. This made it number two on Billboard's album chart in its debut week. The album has twenty-one songs, none of which condone violence. Most are autobiographical and humorous, dealing with topics that many people can relate to. The cover and inside photographs are fun, too. The cover portrays West dressed as a college mascot in a teddy bear suit. West would continue to use a teddy bear as his logo on all his future albums. The inside photos are humorous ones of West as a benched college basketball player, as a loser of a school poetry contest, and as a student who fails to walk across the stage at graduation.

"Jesus Walks"

All the songs on *College Dropout* reveal something about West, and all are full of contradictions. According to journalist Josh Tyrangiel, "*College Dropout* was 76 minutes of someone cramming every thought he'd ever had about himself into rhyme. It was immaculately produced, but what was most compelling was the contradictions.... Throughout West careened between the Protestant ethic and street fantasies, revealing himself to be wise and stupid, arrogant and insecure, often in the same breath."[35]

West performs the controversial "Jesus Walks" at the 2005 Grammy Awards.

One of the most highly publicized and controversial songs on the album is "Jesus Walks." West spent three years working on the tune, which has a religious theme. In it he points out that everyone, including himself, makes mistakes, but that Jesus Christ will forgive them. The song, according to West, "is about imperfection. Everybody can relate to that."[36]

Until "Jesus Walks" hit the market, songs with religious overtones were not popular with hip-hop audiences. Roc-A-Fella had advised West not to record it. Because of its religious nature, it was likely the song would never be played on the radio or in clubs. In fact, in the song West talks about how emcees can rap about violence and hatred without consequence, but if they rap about religion, the song is not played. He then goes on to subtly challenge disc jockeys to play his song because he says the world needs it.

It took confidence and courage for West to go against popular opinion and include "Jesus Walks" on his album. There was a good chance the song would negatively impact sales of *College Dropout* and make West the object of criticism.

West did not care. After his accident, he had become more religious. He thought that God had spared his life so that he could touch people through his music. He believed in the message the song conveyed. And he believed in himself. Ignoring the experts, he recorded "Jesus Walks."

West felt so strongly about the song that he made three different music videos of it, each of which he personally financed. In the first, West plays the role of a rapping minister who helps save the souls of a criminal, a prostitute, and a gangster. In the second, West, along with drug dealers, police, and Ku Klux Klan members, walks beside Jesus Christ. In the third, West and Jesus Christ hang out together in Chicago. Jesus miraculously fills West's empty refrigerator with food and keeps taking a resistant West to church.

Despite predictions to the contrary, "Jesus Walks" was a huge hit. By carefully balancing the song's religious nature with a catchy beat and witty lyrics, West made the song and videos hard to resist. "Jesus Walks" brought a larger and more varied audience to hip-hop music and made it acceptable to talk about God and religion in popular music. Rapper P. Diddy explains, "The way Kanye did it, he made the record so hot.... It's a rap record about Jesus [that] young men and women can understand, instead of you pushing it down their throats. You hit them with that heat and they understood it."[37]

An Award-Winning Year

West's belief in himself and his songs was justified. *College Dropout* was critically acclaimed, as was "Jesus Walks." *Ebony* magazine writer Kimberly Davis called the album "one of the greatest hip-hop albums of all time."[38] While *Rolling Stone* magazine named it their Critics #1 Album of 2004.

Sales of *College Dropout* were so high that it went triple platinum. West had four hit singles off the album. Not only did the album make West extremely rich, but it also brought him the validation as a rapper that he had long sought. In 2005 he was nominated for an unprecedented ten Grammy Awards, topping the number of nominations any artist had previously received. Eight of these nominations were for *College Dropout*. One nomination was for the song, "You Don't Know My Name," which he wrote with Alicia Keys and Harold Lilly, and one was for Best New Artist.

West won three Grammys. *College Dropout* won for Best Rap Album of the Year. "Jesus Walks" won for Best Rap Song of the Year, and "You Don't Know My Name" won for Best R&B Song of the Year. That year West also took home four Billboard music awards, three BET awards, and three MOBO (Music of Black Origin) awards. "Jesus Walks" won the 2005 MTV Video Music Award for Best Male Video. And magazines *Time*, *Rolling Stone*, *Spin*, *Blender*, *GQ*, and the *Source*, and the newspaper, *New York Times*, all named *College Dropout* as their album of the year.

West was now a full-blown star. He performed "Jesus Walks" at the 2005 Grammy Awards, and it was one of the high points of the show. He also appeared on the 4th Annual BET Awards, the 2004 World Music Awards, the MTV Video Music Awards, and on many television talk shows. Plus, he toured with Usher to sold-out audiences. In an interview in *Time* magazine, West explains, "This entire year has been like a roller-coaster ride … I just feel so blessed.… It feels like everybody feels about me like I always felt about myself. I always planned on it. I use to talk [about how good I was] … before I got accolades. People say

Kanye West's Awards

Kanye West has won many prestigious awards. Here is a list of some of them:

2004

Black Entertainment Television (BET): New Artist

MOBO (Music of Black Origin): Best Hip-Hop Artist, Best Producer, Best Album

2005

BET: Best Male Hip-Hop Artist, Video of the Year

Grammy: Best R&B Song, Best Rap Song, Best Rap Album

MTV: Best Male Video

Vibe magazine: Best Rapper

2006

BET: Video of the Year, Best Collaboration, Best Male Hip-Hop Artist

Billboard: Top Rap Album, Hot Rap Track of the Year

BRIT (British Recording Industry): International Male Solo Artist

Grammy: Best Rap Solo Performance, Best Rap Song, Best Rap Album

MTV Europe Music Awards: Best Hip-Hop Act

2007

GQ magazine: International Man of the Year

MOBO: Best Hip-Hop Act, Best Video

Vibe magazine: Mix Tape of the Year

2008

American Music Awards: Favorite Rap/Hip-Hop Album, Favorite Rap/Hip-Hop Male Artist

BET: Best Male Hip-Hop Artist, Best Collaboration

BRIT: International Male Solo Artist

Grammy: Best Rap Solo Performer, Best Rap Performance by a Duo or Group, Best Rap Song, Best Rap Album

MTV Europe Music Awards: Ultimate Urban

MTV: Best Special Effects Video

losing is a humbling experience. No, for me, winning is a humbling experience. I don't have to talk as much because everybody else is saying it for me."[39]

"Touch the Sky"

West came out with his second album, *Late Registration* in August 2005. It debuted as number one on the charts, selling 860,000 copies in its first week and went on to sell more than 3 million copies in all. It garnered multiple awards, including the 2006 Grammy Award for Best Rap Album and Billboard's Top Rap Album. The album had five hit singles. Two songs, "Gold Digger" and "Diamonds Are Forever" won Grammy Awards, BET awards, and Billboard awards. In addition, West received the prestigious Million Man March Image Award, which honored him as an exemplary black man. He was featured on the cover of *Time* magazine, as well as on Barbara Walters' *Most Fascinating People of 2005* television special. He was honored at a special Kanye West Day in Chicago, and he appeared on the *Oprah Winfrey Show*.

The appearance on *Oprah* was especially gratifying for West. Years earlier he had approached Winfrey about appearing on her show. When she turned him down, he confidently predicted that she would have him on her show eventually. And she did.

After years of being rejected, West was finally living his dream. The first song on *Late Registration* is called "Touch the Sky." In it West raps about his life, the rejections he faced, and his ultimate success. He explains,

> "Touch the Sky" is what my life is about.... To anyone that feels like something is so far away [the song is] just the concept of actually being able to leap above the environment that you're in. All the naysayers and haters and people say "You'll never make it that far, you'll never make it out of this town, we'll call you," and all those things, and finally you get the opportunity to touch the sky . . . so no matter what they give me or try to take from me, there's nothing you can take from me. We've already touched the sky. With or without any accolades, whatever it is, the fact that people listen to this music and it's connected with people, the fact that you

At the 48th Annual Grammy Awards, West won Best Rap Solo Performance for "Gold Digger," Best Rap Song for "Diamonds From Sierra Leone," and Best Rap Album for "Late Registration."

see fans crying in the audience—you can't tell me anything after that because there's so many places and establishments where people are out of touch. When someone hears your songs and cries, then you're in touch and that's what matters. At that point, you feel you've touched the sky.[40]

Getting Out Our Dreams

West added to his success with his third album *Graduation*, which won him three more Grammy Awards, including Best Rap Album. By the close of 2008, he had won thirty-six different awards and had been nominated for a total of 112 awards, including six 2009 Grammy Awards. In just a few years West had become richer and more successful than even he had predicted.

Many Activities

Besides his musical career and his work in fashion design, Kanye West is involved in a number of other activities. In June 2008 he launched his own search engine, www.search-withkanye.com. Visitors to the site get "swag bucks," rewards that can be used to buy West's autographed CDs and exclusive clothing and other merchandise. West has also launched his own travel Web site, www.kanyetravel.com. The site offers travel packages and tickets to his shows.

West also appears in movies and on television shows. He has had roles in the movies *The Love Guru*, *State Property II*, and *Fade to Black*, and he has been featured on the television shows *Saturday Night Live*, the *Ellen DeGeneres Show*, *Good Morning America*, the *Tonight Show*, the *Today Show*, *Entourage*, *Cribs*, *Late Night with Conan O'Brien*, and the *Late Show with David Letterman*. West is also currently developing a comedy series for HBO based on his childhood.

Although much of his success was due to his own natural talent and determination, he was grateful to musicians like Jay-Z and No I.D. who had helped him along the way. In order to help other musicians, he started his own record label, Getting Out Our Dreams (G.O.O.D Music) in 2004. He explains, "I didn't even want to do the label thing.... I just did it to give people the opportunity to get their dreams out. That's why it's called Getting Out Our Dreams.... I just think it is a dope way to springboard [a good way to introduce] all these artists that the world needs to hear."[41]

The first person West signed was his longtime friend COMMON, whose career had been on the decline. Recording with West helped change that. COMMON explains,

> I got to attribute a lot to Kanye. He pushed me as an artist. He made music that was incredible ... that was me, but the masses could still touch down with it. He came with ideas and choruses so I got to give him credit, man. The dude is a genius.... Not only do I love Kanye creatively and as a brother ... but we doing business with a vision ... and we're making each other wealthier.[42]

West also signed a number of new artists, including Consequence, Sa-Ra, GLC, Farnsworth Bentley, and John Legend. West has proven himself to be a shrewd businessman and a wise judge of talent. G.O.O.D. Music is quite successful, as are its artists. Indeed, the albums Legend recorded on the label garnered the singer five Grammy Awards. Legend readily admits that West has had a big impact on his success.

Fashion Trendsetter and Businessman

G.O.O.D. Music is not West's only business enterprise. His life-long love of art, design, and fashion and the popularity of the way he dresses led him to a second career in fashion design. West's unique sense of style, which was once considered a negative by

Designer Marc Jacobs holds the shoe West designed for Louis Vuitton in 2009. The rapper also designed sunglasses for Vuitton and came out with his own clothing line in 2008.

music industry executives, has proven to be almost as popular as his music. West has been named to many best-dressed lists and was *Stuff* magazine's 2005 Style Icon of the Year.

West has become a fashion role model for young people. From the start, his fans so admired his fashion sense that they copied it. Pastel polo shirts and khaki pants have become as popular with hip-hop audiences as oversized team shirts and baggy pants.

West's clothing line, Pastelle, debuted in 2008. He is also involved in designing sunglasses. And he has collaborated with Louis Vuitton on jewelry and men's shoe designs. West takes his work as a fashion designer quite seriously. "I wanted to be a fashion designer since before I wanted to be a rapper," he explains. "Nobody said I could be a rapper and now I'm the be-all and end-all of rap. Next, I'm gonna be the be-all and end-all of fashion."[43]

Tragedy Strikes

West shared all of his successes in music and business with his mother. Through adversity and triumph, she was his greatest fan, most loyal supporter, and best friend. In 2004 West made Donda his business manager. When he moved to Los Angeles, California, he bought his mother a large home close to his own, as well as a brand-new Mercedes-Benz.

In November 2007 Donda underwent cosmetic surgery. One day later, she suddenly died from heart failure. The cause of her heart failure is still uncertain. West was in Europe at the time, preparing for a concert tour there. He was overwhelmed by her unexpected death. Many individuals advised him to take time off from his work to grieve. Instead, he continued touring. He felt it was what his mother would have wanted him to do. Speaking from the stage in Brussels, Belgium, a week after her death, West said,

West kisses mom Donda at a post-Grammy party in early 2007. Later that year she died of heart failure after having cosmetic surgery.

There's nothing that she loved more than to come to the shows and scream louder than any fan. Because she was my first fan that was screaming before anyone else. My first manager. And if she was here, she would tell me to "get on that stage and kill it dawg." ... She would tell me to go on this ... tour and take over the world and "Be number one like how I taught you to be baby."[44]

Continuing the tour was not easy. In his first concert after her death, West tried to sing "Hey Mama" and broke down in tears. He left the stage in order to get control of his emotions, then came back to perform a moving rendition of "Stronger." A year later he did manage to perform "Hey Mama," dedicated to his mother, at the 2008 Grammy Awards.

Although dealing with his mother's death has been difficult for West, working helped him to cope. The suddenness of her death also made him more philosophical about his own life and the direction it was taking. Even in death, West's mother still had something to teach him about living his life. He put it this way on his blog:

I don't do anything I don't love anymore. While people chase money, I pursue happiness. So many people talk about their investments or how much money they have but there's so many rich people who spend a lot of that trying 2 buy a piece of happiness. If there's anything my mom taught me it is to enjoy life.... [Music video director] Chris Milk told me tragedy can produce great art and that is definitely true. I am a total mad man now, up til 3 am every night, trying 2 fight pain, board-um, and uncertainty with creativity. All that said, life is good.[45]

Chapter 5

Speaking Out

Kanye West has never been afraid to speak his mind. Becoming a superstar has not changed that. His outspokenness, whether about social issues or about himself, has led to criticism and controversy. That has not stopped West from speaking the truth as he sees it, no matter the consequences. Indeed, some experts say his openness has added to his success. West puts it this way: "I'm an artist that people love to hate. Even if they love me sometimes they like to talk … about me, because there are very few artists who stand up for what they believe in."[46]

Confidence or Arrogance?

West's outspokenness about his talent has led to the most criticism. He has called himself the number-one musical artist in the world and the voice of his generation. In 2007 he told radio interviewer Wendy Williams, "I'm the number one artist in the world right now…. I am the number one human being in music. That means that any person that's living or breathing is number two…. People got to look at the concerts, look at the sales, look at the impact, look at the songs, look at the connection with pop culture. I mean it's obvious."[47]

Some people interpret West's belief in himself and his music as arrogance. West insists he is just being honest. He says,

> To go gold or platinum, to have songs that are respected across the board, to have some sort of influence on the culture and

He Said What?

Kanye West has spoken out about many things during his career. Some of his statements seem to be overly confident, while others reveal his insecurities. Others are quite philosophical. These are a few of his most well-known:

"My music isn't just music–it's medicine."

"In America, they want you to accomplish these great feats, to pull off these David Copperfield-type [a magician] stunts. You want me to be great, but you don't ever want me to say I'm great?"

"We [are] all self-conscious. I'm just the first to admit it."

"If I was more complacent and I let things slide, my life would be easier, but you all wouldn't be as entertained. My misery is your pleasure."

"If you have the opportunity to play this game of life you need to appreciate every moment. A lot of people don't appreciate the moment until it's passed."

"Nothing in life is promised except death."

Finest Quotes, "Kanye West Quotes," www.finestquotes.com/author_quotes-author-Kanye%20West-page-0.htm.

change the sound of music and inspire up-and-coming artists to go against the grain. If I was to say that I hadn't already done all of that, then I'd be on some fake Hollywood … modesty, and that's just plain stupid.[48]

West is so passionate about the quality of his work that he has been known to blurt out whatever is in his heart even when it is impolite to do so. In 2004, for example, when he was not named the American Music Awards Best New Artist, he told reporters, "I felt like I was definitely robbed, and I refused to give any politically correct … comment. I was the best new artist of the year."[49]

In 2006 when "Touch the Sky" did not win the MTV European Music Video of the Year Award, West stormed the stage and interrupted the winners', Justice and Simian's, acceptance speech.

In 2006 when "Touch the Sky" did not win the MTV European Music Video of the Year Award, West stormed the stage and interrupted the winners', Justice and Simian's, acceptance speech. He announced that he should have won. Backstage, he told the press, "It's complete bullshit, I paid a million dollars [to make the video].... It took a month to film; I stood on a mountain; I flew a helicopter over Vegas.... I did it to be the king of all videos."⁵⁰

Even before an award is presented, West has something to say. For instance, a week before the 2006 Grammy nominations were announced, he told MTV:

If I don't win Album of the Year, I'm gonna really have a problem with that. I can never talk myself out of [winning], you know why? Because I put in the work. I don't care if I jumped up and down on the couch like Tom Cruise. I don't care what I do, I don't care how much I stunt—you can never take away from the amount of work I put into it.... You put the camera in front of me, I'm gonna tell you like this. I worked hard to get here. I put my love, I put my heart, I put my money [into *Late Registration*].... People love these songs.... I said I was the face of the Grammy's last year. I'm 10 times that [this year].[51]

West readily admits that sometimes he oversteps polite boundaries, and he even raps about it in his song, "Can't Tell Me Nothing," where he says that sometimes he acts recklessly and stupidly.

Yet, it is unlikely that West will stop speaking out about his work. He is too passionate about it to remain silent. "My music isn't just music—it's a medicine. Every time I make an album I'm trying to make a cure for cancer 'musically,'"[52] he explains.

Hurricane Katrina

West also raises eyebrows when he speaks out about social issues. Many of his songs tackle controversial issues, like the plight of diamond miners in South Africa, sexual abuse of women, racism, and rampant materialism. He has also spoken out nonmusically. After Hurricane Katrina devastated New Orleans, Louisiana, in 2005, West, along with many other celebrities, appeared on *Concert for Hurricane Relief*, a live telethon broadcast on NBC. His impromptu comments at this event created quite a controversy.

West was supposed to read a statement from a script, which described the destruction that the hurricane caused. Instead of following the script, he spoke from his heart and said:

I hate the way they portray us [black people] in the media. You see a black family, it says "they're looting." You see a white family, it says, "They're looking for food." And, you know, it's been five days [without federal help arriving in New Orleans] because most of the people are black. And

When West saw the devastation caused by Hurricane Katrina, like this neighborhood in Biloxi, Mississippi, he openly criticized the way the U.S. government was handling support.

even for me to complain about it, I would be a hypocrite because I've tried to turn away from the TV because it's too hard to watch, I've even been shopping before even giving a donation, so now I'm calling my business manager right now to see what is the biggest amount I can give, and just to imagine if I was down there, and those are my people down there. So anybody out there that wants to do anything that can help—with the way America is set up to help the poor, the black people, the less well-off, as slow as possible. I mean, the Red Cross, is doing everything they can.... [Former president] George Bush doesn't care about black people![53]

At that point, NBC cut away from West. The network feared West's comments would politicize the telethon, and it wanted to distance itself from him. Because the program was being aired live on the East Coast, the network could not edit out West's speech there. They did cut it from the other time zones and quickly issued a statement that the rapper's comments did not reflect the opinions of the network or of the other celebrities present.

West's speech did cause a stir. Some Americans applauded him. His longtime friend and fellow rapper, Rhymefest, called West a hero for saying what many other people, including himself, were afraid to say. Reverend Al Sharpton thanked West for saying what needed to be said. And actor Matt Damon publicly supported him. Other people were not as enthusiastic. West's words angered many individuals. His former concert partner, Usher, for example, publicly condemned West for his statement.

West lost a number of musical jobs because of his speech, and he was poorly received at some performances. When he performed remotely at the New England Patriots 2005 home opener game, he was booed so loudly that it was difficult to hear his song.

None of this surprised West. He knew what he had said would be controversial and could damage, or even end, his career. When he started to speak, he appeared nervous and his voice was shaking. But he was raised to speak his mind and do what he could to right social wrongs. So he did not back down.

Despite the personal consequences, he said what he felt needed to be said.

A few months later journalist Barbara Walters asked West in an interview if he regretted his speech. He assured her that he had no regrets because he had spoken from his heart.

Speaking Out Against Homophobia

West also spoke from his heart when he spoke out against the unfair treatment of gays. Rap lyrics often disrespect gays. Being labeled gay or having gay friends can ruin a hip-hop artist's career. Traditionally, a dislike for gays is widespread in hip-hop culture. This may be because most rap stars try to project an ultra-masculine, tough-guy image, and almost all categorize themselves as heterosexuals. West readily admits that while trying to make it as a rapper, he said negative things about and discriminated against homosexuals to protect his career. When West's cousin admitted he was a homosexual, West realized that his behavior and the behavior of other hip-hop artists was wrong. He recalls, "It was kind of like a turning point when I was like, 'Yo, this is my cousin. I love him and I've been discriminating against gays.'"[54]

West immediately changed his own attitude toward homosexuals. But that was not enough for him. Once again he spoke publicly about a wrong that he felt needed righting. Doing so meant criticizing his peers and the industry he depended on. West knew his position would not be popular. Indeed, it could have been the end of his career. Yet, he still spoke out. He explains,

> I actually think that standing up for gays was even more crazy than bad-mouthing the president. In the black community someone could label you gay and bring your career down. But that was me showing what black people are really about today, or at least what we need to be about.... When you stand up for any form of civil rights, you put yourself in the line of fire. But I feel like I'm here to change people's hearts and minds, to say something that's right for a change. And it goes all the way down the line, from telling people to stop being so cliché, to stop saying what you think your record label wants you to say, to stop giving drab acceptance speeches. Speaking from the heart is so much more entertaining.[55]

Dr. Donda West Foundation

West not only speaks from his heart, but he also acts from it. In 2003 he and his mother founded the Kanye West Foundation. West changed the name of the foundation to the Dr. Donda West

Foundation in 2008 as a tribute to his mother. It is a charitable organization aimed at decreasing the high school dropout rate in schools throughout the United States. It does this through a program called Loop Dreams.

Loop Dreams uses young people's interest in hip-hop to motivate them to stay in school. As part of the program, participants learn about different careers in music. They learn how to write music and lyrics, use production equipment, operate stage lights, and produce a demo tape, among other things. In order to participate in the program, students must stay in school and maintain good grades. To help them do this, Loop Dreams provides

A crowd gathers outside the Creative Artist Agency Foundation launch of the Kanye West Foundation. West changed the name of the foundation to the Dr. Donda West Foundation in 2008 as a tribute to his mother.

participants with academic tutoring. According to an article on the foundation's Web site,

> to Kanye, superstar status carries with it responsibility. It mandates giving back to the world community in proportion to what he has received.... The Loop Dreams program opens students' minds to creativity, taps into their unlimited potential, and motivates them to remain focused on the importance of education.... It is Kanye's vision and the vision of the foundation that through "Loop Dreams", kids who might otherwise dropout of school and face dismal futures, will instead remain in school, graduate, and pursue options allowing them to contribute positively to the world, and to lead enriched, productive, and fulfilled lives.[56]

Currently, the Loop Dreams program is operating in California. West hopes to expand the program to other states soon. In addition, the foundation has done international work by donating books and school supplies to schools in Sierra Leone, Africa. It has also helped provide nutritional support to schoolchildren in Sierra Leone's diamond-mining region.

West is personally involved in raising money for the foundation. He has done charity concerts and organized fundraisers for it. One event that he arranged was a silent auction in which his own personal items were sold to fund the foundation.

Helping Veterans

West has also given his support to veterans returning from the wars in Afghanistan and Iraq. In conversations with servicemen and women, MTV News learned that many of the troops in Iraq and Afghanistan listen to West's music as a way to relieve stress and connect with home. When these young men and women return to the United States, they often have trouble adjusting. Many must cope with financial problems and post-traumatic stress disorder, an emotional illness that occurs as a result of a life-threatening experience.

When West learned about the impact his music is having on these brave men and women and about the problems they face

Good Water Store Café

There are more than 1 billion people in the world without a sufficient water supply. More than 2.4 billion lack basic sanitation. Many die from preventable water-related diseases, including thousands of children. Kanye West and his father are concerned about the plight of these people. They have been working to help fund projects that provide people with water.

In 2007 they supported a World Water Day event in which they helped sponsor a Walk for Water rally. In 2008 they opened the Good Water Store Café in Washington, D.C. The café serves drinks that are made with all fresh and natural ingredients and sells purified water. It also serves as a community center with a play area for children, comfortable chairs for reading, and a stage for community productions. The café also provides a place where patrons can learn more about the world water problem and what they can do to help.

after returning home, he wanted to express his gratitude to them. In 2008 he teamed up with MTV in order to give three veterans an unforgettable homecoming. He visited their homes bearing gifts, which were paid for by his foundation. The gifts included debt assistance, rent, a college tuition fund, and musical equipment. And he gave each veteran a private concert.

He also talked with the veterans about their experiences in the Middle East and the problems they face in readjusting to life in the United States. Their discussions were filmed and shown on *Kanye West Presents: Homecoming*, an MTV special program, which aired in July 2008. West explains,

There are hundreds of veterans out there who are falling through the cracks. They make the ultimate sacrifices for us by laying down their lives, but it seems like a lot of them just got forgotten about. I know my music inspires and helps a lot of people, but you can always do more. I teamed up with MTV and took the opportunity to share the spotlight with these veterans and hear their stories. I went to their homes to listen and get their firsthand experiences. I wanted to hear their stories.[57]

Into the Future

West's rise to fame has certainly been stunning. Despite the fact that industry experts doubted it could happen, he became a hip-hop superstar while remaining true to himself.

No one knows what the future holds for West. When it comes to his personal life, he readily admits that he is still getting over the loss of his mother. He is also dealing with a failed romantic relationship. He became engaged to fashion designer, Alexis Phifer in 2006. The two had been dating since 2002. In 2008 their relationship fell apart, which saddened West. He insists that he is ready to get married and start a family, and he hopes to find someone to spend the rest of his life with soon.

Musically, he continues to work and his newest CD reflects, as usual, his life. *808s & Heartbreak* was released in November 2008. It is different from his earlier work in that West sings more than he raps. The melodies, too, have a different, more mainstream sound. The songs are all quite emotional, reflecting all he's gone through in the past few years. Many deal with loneliness. "Coldest Winter," for instance, is an emotionally charged song that he dedicated to his mother. "Welcome to Heartbreak" also deals with loneliness, specifically West's single status and his desire to start of family. Although the CD has received good reviews, some members of the hip-hop community say that West has lost direction. Because West sings rather than raps, because the melodies are different, and because the subject matter is so emotionally raw, they say he has crossed over into pop music. West disagrees. The tracks, he says, were

just what was in my heart. The type of ideas that I was coming up with, they were melodies that were in me—what

West and fiance Alexis Phifer toast at a private dinner party in New York, 2007. The couple dated since 2002 but broke up in 2008.

was in me I couldn't stop. I think it's a path; it's a road that's been paved and given by God … I just have to follow the signs and arrows of where he wants me to go and just be fearless about it. It's so crazy—hip-hop used to be about being fearless, and now it's, like, all about being afraid. It used to be about standing out, and now it's all about fitting in. Like, you know, I wear my tight jeans and stuff and stand out and people want to talk about me. Now hip-hop is like a big high school or something—so that's why I respect people who just do whatever they want to do.[58]

No matter where the future takes him, one thing is likely. West will proceed fearlessly, and he will do whatever he wants to do. He has talked about taking time off from his musical career to study fashion design. He is also quite interested in architecture and interior design, as well as becoming a television actor.

And he is very involved with his foundation. With all his talent, there are many paths he can follow. Since he has never been afraid to be different, he is likely to surprise the world with what he does next. His confidence, outspokenness, and faith in himself have taken him far. He has always said what was on his mind and fought for what he believed in. No matter what direction he takes next, it is clear that he will continue to be his own person and follow his heart.

Introduction: Music for Everyone

1. Quoted in Josh Tyrangiel, "Why You Can't Ignore Kanye," *Time*, August 21, 2005, www.time.com/time/magazine/article/0,9171,1096499,00.html.
2. Jake Brown, *Kanye West in the Studio*. Phoenix, AZ: Colossus, 2006, p. 9.
3. Quoted in Brown, *Kanye West in the Studio*, p. 10.
4. Quoted in Artist Direct, "Kanye West Biography," Artist Direct, www.artistdirect.com/nad/music/artist/bio/0,,721308,00.html.
5. Brown, *Kanye West in the Studio*, p. 35.
6. Quoted in Artist Direct, "Kanye West Biography."
7. Walt Mueller, "Kanye West: The Dropout Drops In," YouthMinistry.com, August 23, 2007, www.youthministry.com/?q=node/4835.

Chapter 1: A Strong Influence

8. Donda West, *Raising Kanye*. New York: Pocket, 2007, p. 46.
9. West, *Raising Kanye*, p. 71.
10. Quoted in Kimberly Davis, "Kanye West Hip-Hop's New Big Shot," *Ebony*, April 2005, p. 156.
11. West, *Raising Kanye*, p. 4.
12. Quoted in Shaheem Reid, "Kanye West Has Paid Tribute to His Mom Donda, Throughout His Career—In Songs and Interviews," MTV, November 13, 2007, www.mtv.com/news/articles/1574107/20071112/west_kanye.jhtml.
13. Quoted in Luke Bainbridge, "It's Kanye's World," *Observer*, August 12, 2007, www.guardian.co.uk/music/2007/aug/12/urban.kanyewest.
14. Quoted in Telegraph.co uk, "Inside Tracks: Told to the Telegraph," December 30, 2004, www.telegraph.co.uk/culture/3634100/Inside-tracks-Told-to-the-telegraph.html.
15. Quoted in Brown, *Kanye West in the Studio*, p. 20.

Chapter 2: Following His Dream

16. West, *Raising Kanye*, p. 105.
17. Quoted in Brown, *Kanye West in the Studio*, p. 30.
18. No I.D., *Kanye West Mentor No I.D.*, YouTube video, September 26, 2007, www.youtube.com/watch?v=nDpr9 jlw5oI&feature=related.
19. Quoted in Barbara Kiviat, "10 Questions for Kanye West," *Time*, December 20, 2004, p. 8.
20. Quoted in Greg Kot, "Rapper's Rise: From South Side to Top of the Charts," *Chicago Tribune*, February 11, 2004, www. rocafella.com/News.aspx?item=101084&sectionid=137.
21. Quoted in Brown, *Kanye West in the Studio*, p. 22.
22. West, *Raising Kanye*, p. 118.

Chapter 3: More Than a Producer

23. Quoted in Kot, "Rapper's Rise."
24. Quoted in Brown, *Kanye West in the Studio*, p. 25.
25. Quoted in Simon Vozick-Levinson, "Jay-Z's Brotherly Love," EW.com, September 18, 2007, www.ew.com/ew/ article/0,,20057568,00.html.
26. Shaheem Reid, "My First Meeting with Kanye West," MTV, November 20, 2008, http://newsroom.mtv.com/2008/11/20/ my-first-meeting-with-kanye-west.
27. Quoted in Andrew Dansby, "Kanye Drops with ODB, Mos Def," *Rolling Stone*, October 28, 2003, www.rollingstone. com/artists/kanyewest/articles/story/5936952/kanye_ drops_with_odb_mos_def.
28. Quoted in Tyrangiel, "Why You Can't Ignore Kanye."
29. Quoted in Tyrangiel, "Why You Can't Ignore Kanye."
30. Quoted in Karen Valby, "The Ego Has Landed," EW.com, January 25, 2006, www.ew.com/ew/article/0,,526091_0_ 1152908,00.html.
31. West, *Raising Kanye*, p. 121.
32. Quoted in Brown, *Kanye West in the Studio*, p. 27.
33. Quoted in Jody Rosen, "Way Out West," Blender.com, September 18, 2007, www.blender.com/guide/articles. aspx?id=2850.

34. Quoted in JamBase, "Kanye West," JamBase, www.jambase. com/Artists/23036/Kanye-West/Bio.

Chapter 4: Superstar

35. Tyrangiel, "Why You Can't Ignore Kanye."
36. Quoted in Tyrangiel, "Why You Can't Ignore Kanye."
37. Quoted in Shaheem Reid, Corey Moss, and Curtis Waller, "Finding My Religion," MTV, www.mtv.com/bands/h/hip_ hop_religion/news_feature_071904.
38. Davis, "Kanye West Hip-Hop's New Big Shot," p. 156.
39. Quoted in Kiviat, "10 Questions for Kanye West," p. 8.
40. Quoted in Corey Moss, "Kanye's at It Again: 'If I Don't Win Album of the Year, I'm Gonna Have a Problem,'" MTV, December 6, 2005, www.mtv.com/news/articles/ 1517545/2005/1206/west_kanye.jhtml.
41. Quoted in Brown, *Kanye West in the Studio*, p. 67.
42. Quoted in Brown, *Kanye West in the Studio*, p. 110.
43. Quoted in Jonathan S. Paul, "Live from Colette: Kanye West," Moment, February 28, 2008, http://themoment.blogs. nytimes.com/2008/02/28/live-from-colette-kanye-west.
44. Quoted in *People*, "Kanye West: My Mom Was My First Fan," *People*, November 20, 2007, www.people.com/people/ article/0,,20161641,00.html.
45. Kanye West, "2008-04-14," KanYe West, www.kanye.ws/ news/html.

Chapter 5: Speaking Out

46. Quoted in Bainbridge, "It's Kanye's World."
47. Quoted in Chris Heath, "Men of the Year: Graduate," Men. Style.com, http://men.style.com/gq/features/landing?id= content_6201.
48. Quoted in Lola Ogunnaike, "Kanye West World," *Rolling Stone*, January 25, 2006, www.rollingstone.com/news/ story/9183008/cover_story_kanye_west_world.
49. Quoted in James Montgomery, "Heard Him Say! A Timeline of Kanye West's Public Outbursts," MTV, September 12, 2007, www.mtv.com/news/articles/1569536/20070912/ west_kanye.jhtml.

50. Quoted in Montgomery, "Heard Him Say!"
51. Quoted in Moss, "Kanye's at It Again."
52. Quoted in Dansby, "Kanye Drops with ODB, Mos Def."
53. Quoted in Lisa de Moraes, "Kanye West's Torrent of Criticism, Live on NBC," *Washington Post*, September 3, 2005, www.washingtonpost.com/wp-dyn/content/article/2005/09/03/AR2005090300165.html.
54. Quoted in *USA Today*, "Kanye West Calls for End to Gay Bashing," *USA Today*, August 18, 2005, www.usatoday.com/life/people/2005-08-18-kanye-west_x.htm?cap=34.
55. Quoted in Valby, "The Ego Has Landed."
56. Kanye West Foundation, "Loop Dreams," www.drdondawest-foundation.org/loop_dreams.html.
57. Quoted in Danielle Harling, "Kanye West Surprises Vets with a Concert," HipHop DX, July 22, 2008, http://cdn.hiphopdx.com/index/news/id.7360/title.kanye-west-surprises-vets-with-a-concert.
58. Quoted in Shaheem Reid, "Kanye West Focuses on Melodies on 'Minimal But Functional' *808s & Heartbreak*," MTV, November 19, 2008, www.mtv.com/news/articles/1599782/2081119/west_kanye.jhtml.

1977

Kanye Omari West is born on June 8 in Atlanta, Georgia.

1980

West's parents divorce. He and his mother move to Chicago.

1987

West and his mother live in China for a year.

1989

West writes and records his first song, "Green Eggs and Ham."

1995

West graduates from high school.

1996

West drops out of college and starts producing songs.

2001

West moves to the New York area and produces tracks for Jay-Z's album, *The Blueprint*.

2002

West signs with Roc-A-Fella Records and records "Through the Wire." He is in a near-fatal car accident in Los Angeles, California.

2004

College Dropout is released.

2005

West wins three Grammys and starts G.O.O.D. Music. *Late Registration* is released.

2006

West wins three Grammys. He becomes engaged to Alexis Phifer.

2007

Graduation is released. Donda West dies.

2008

West wins four Grammys, and his Pastelle fashion line debuts. *808s & Heartbreak* is released. He and Phifer break up.

For More Information

Books

Rae Simons, *Kanye West*. Broomall, PA: Mason Crest, 2008. A biography about Kanye West with colorful photos, this book is written for young adults.

Rosa Waters, *Hip Hop: A Short History*. Broomall, PA: Mason Crest, 2007. This book talks about the origins and growth of hip-hop music and culture with colorful pictures and a timeline.

Gretchen Weicker, *Kanye West: Hip-Hop Star*. Berkeley Heights, NJ: Enslow, 2009. A simple biography about West.

Peggy Sue Wells, *Kanye West*. Hockessin, DE: Mitchell Lane, 2009. This is a short biography about Kanye West for young adults.

Internet Sources

Josh Tyrangiel, "Why You Can't Ignore Kanye," *Time*, August 21, 2005, www.time.com/time/magazine/article/0,9171,1096499,00.html.

Karen Valby, "The Ego Has Landed," EW.com, January 25, 2006, www.ew.com/ew/article/0,,526091_0_1152908,00.html.

Periodicals

Christian Hoard, "New Faces: Kanye West," Rolling Stone, November 18, 2003.

Kelefa Sanneh, "Critic's Choice/ New CD's: No Reading and Writing, But Rapping Instead," *New York Times*, February 9, 2004

Austin Skaggs, "Kanye: A Genius in Praise of Himself, *Rolling Stone*, September 20, 2007.

Brian Stelter, "Kanye's MTV Homecoming Special," *New York Times*, July 28, 2008.

Web Sites

Dr. Donda West Foundation (www.kanyewestfoundation.org). The foundation helps young people stay in school and teaches them about the recording industry. The website provides information about upcoming fundraising events including concerts, a recorded message from Kanye, and contact information.

KanyeUniverseCity.com (www.kanyeuniversecity.com). This is Kanye West's official Web site, and it includes his personal blog, news, videos, photos, and merchandise.

Barbara Sheen is the author of more than forty books for young people. She lives in New Mexico with her family. In her spare time she likes to swim, walk, cook, weight train, and garden.